Meditative Mandalas

A Hand Drawn Coloring Book

Bala Thiagarajan, Ph.D

ArtbyBala.com
facebook.com/ArtbyBala

Cover Image - Elyse O'Brien

ISBN: 1979988609
ISBN-13: 978-1979988605

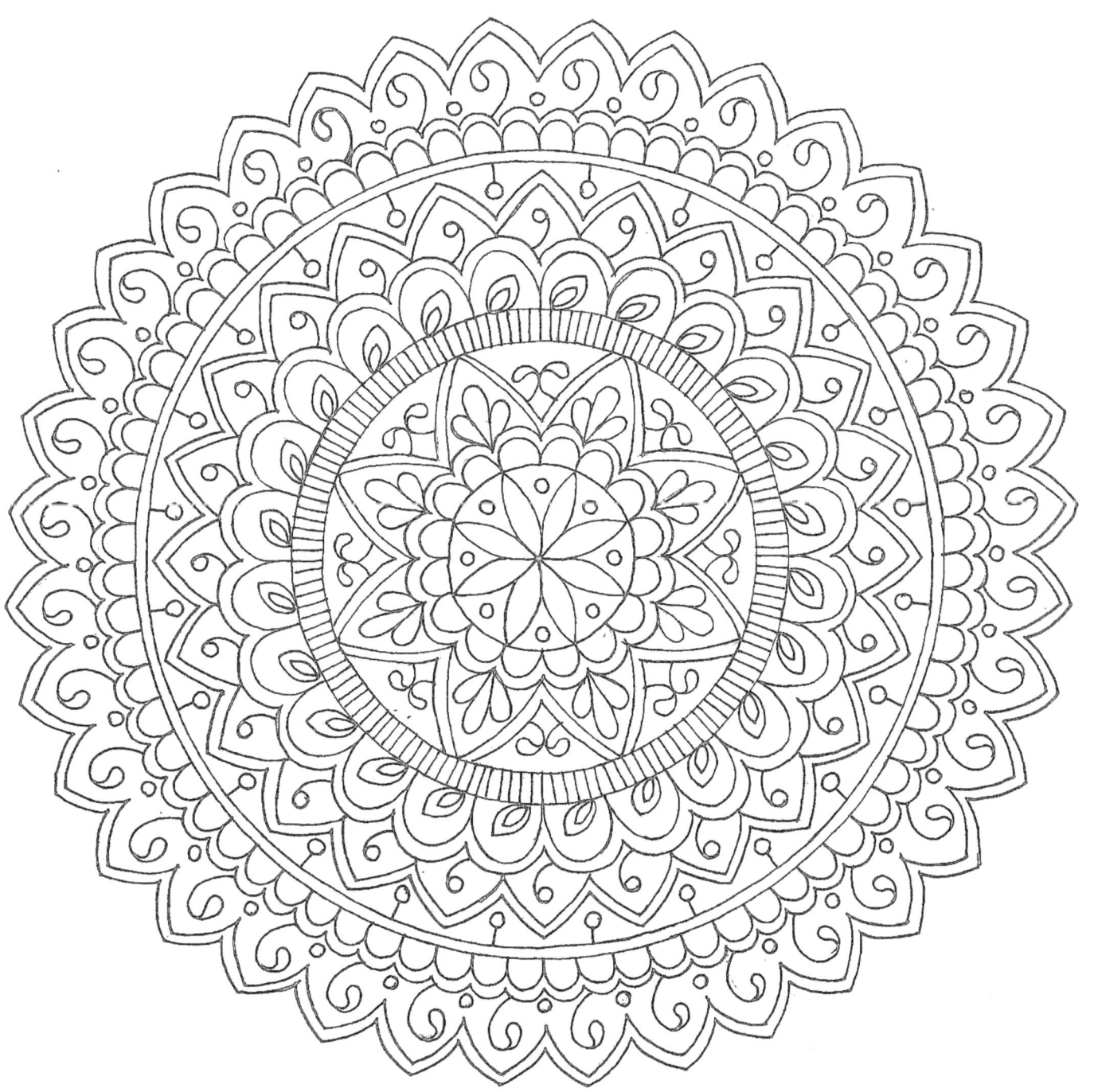

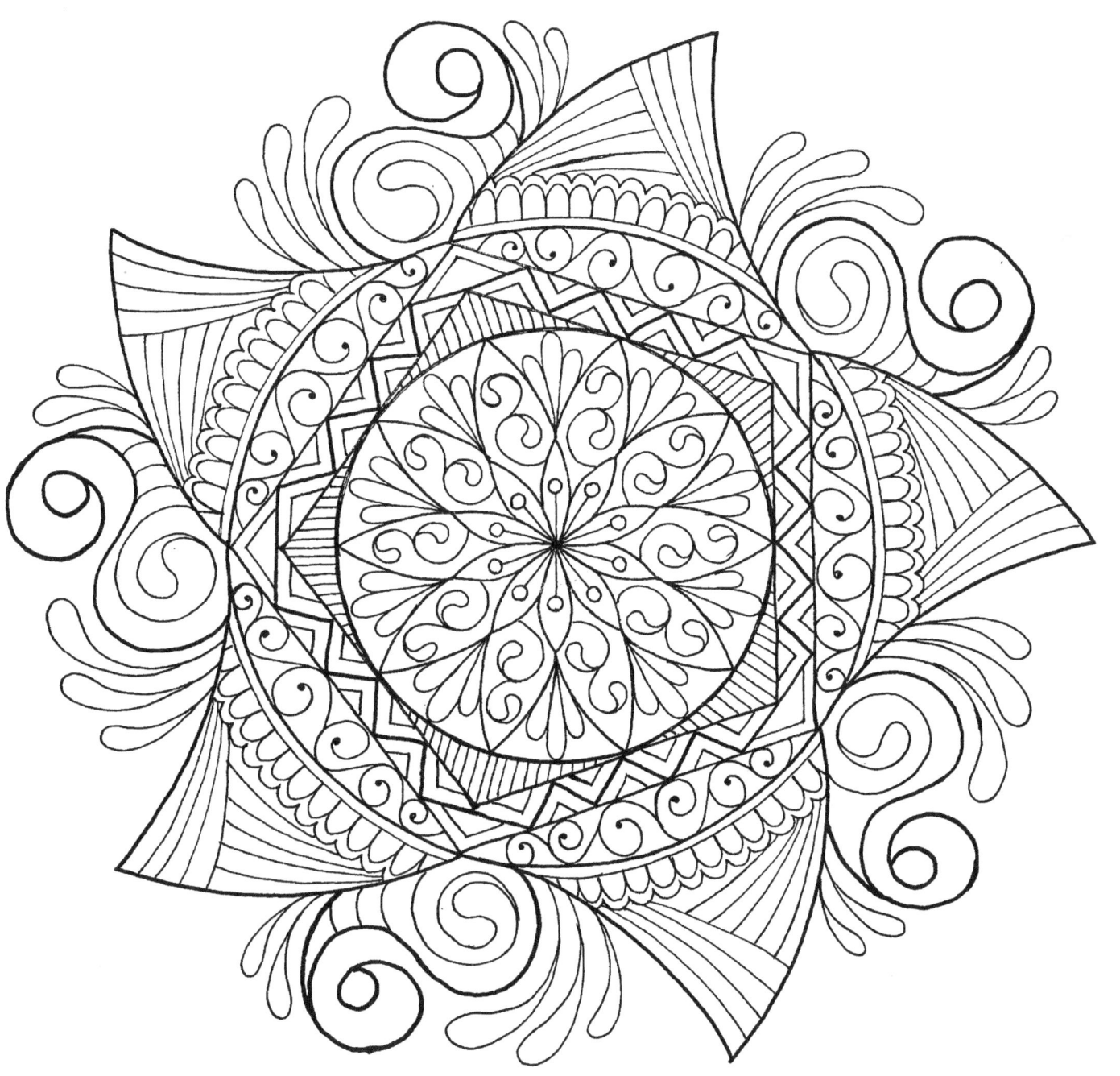

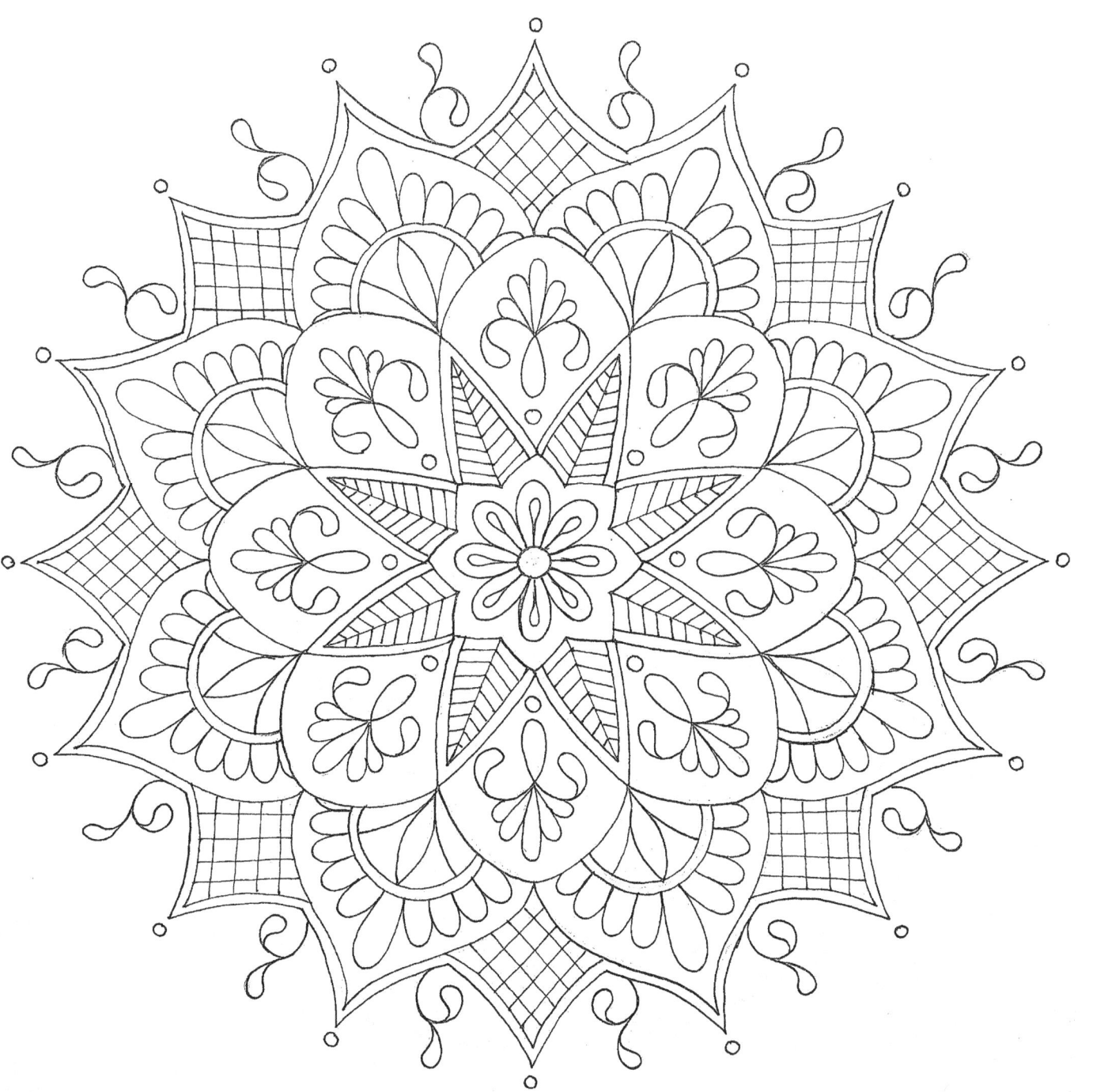

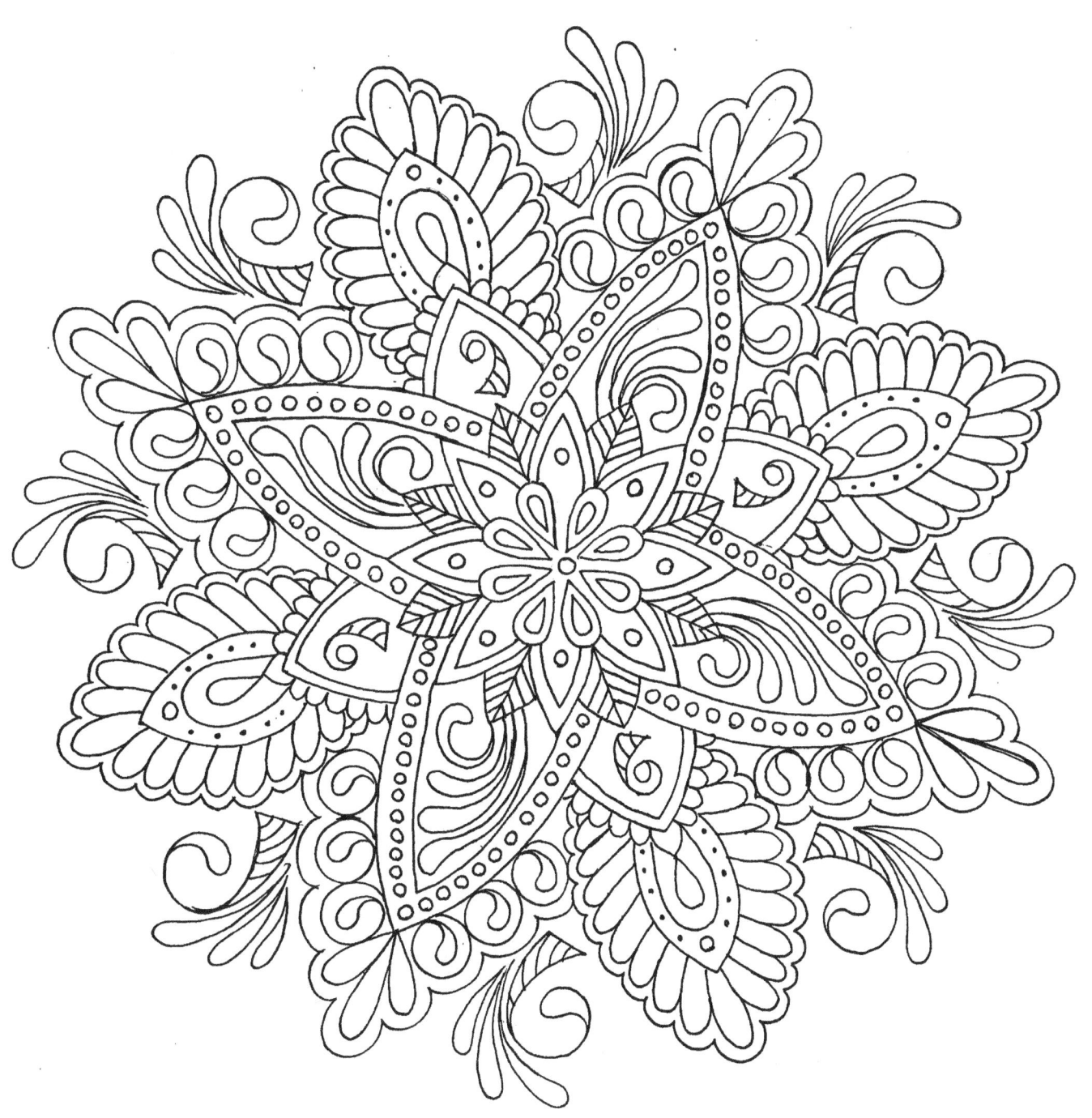

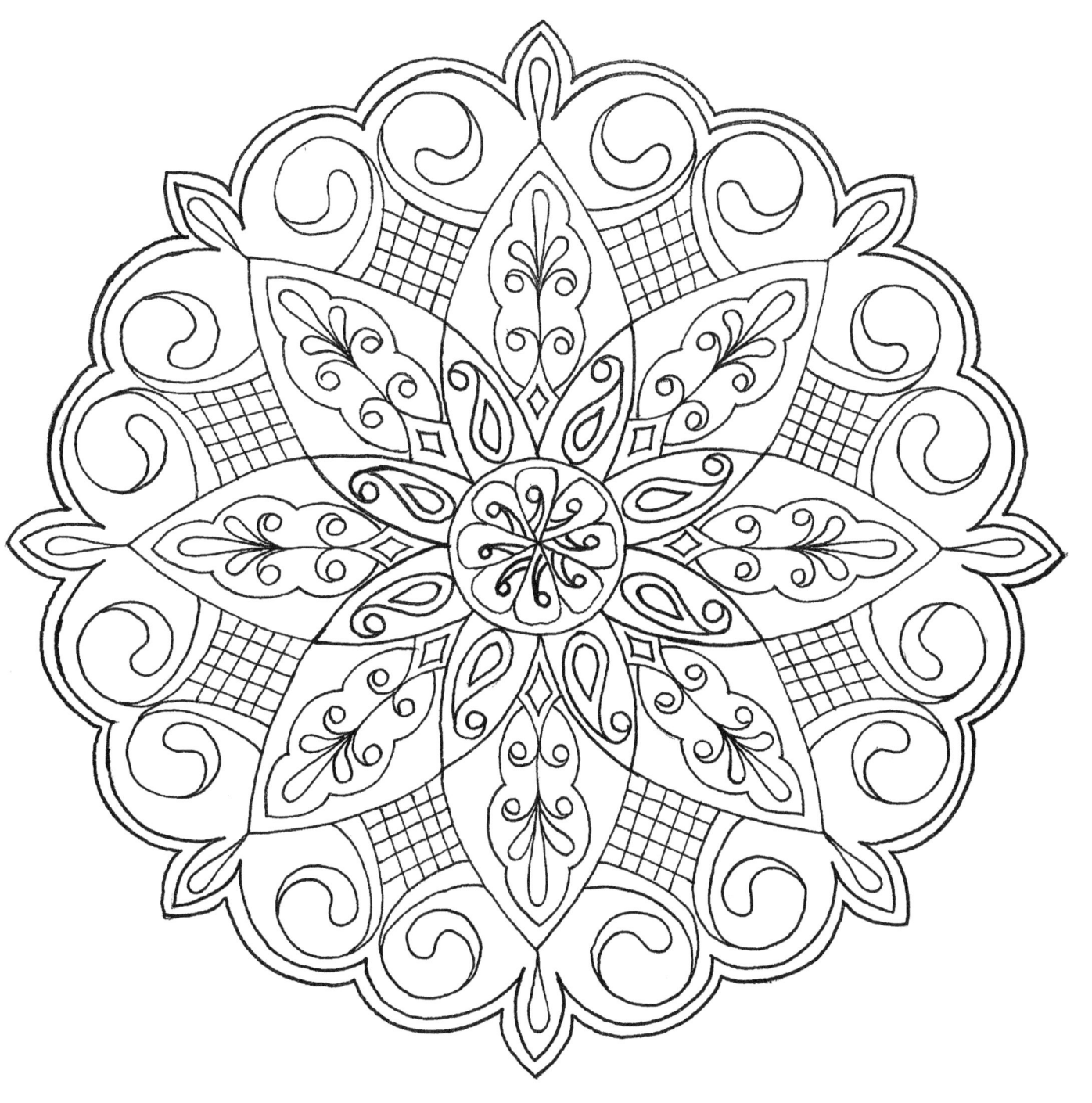

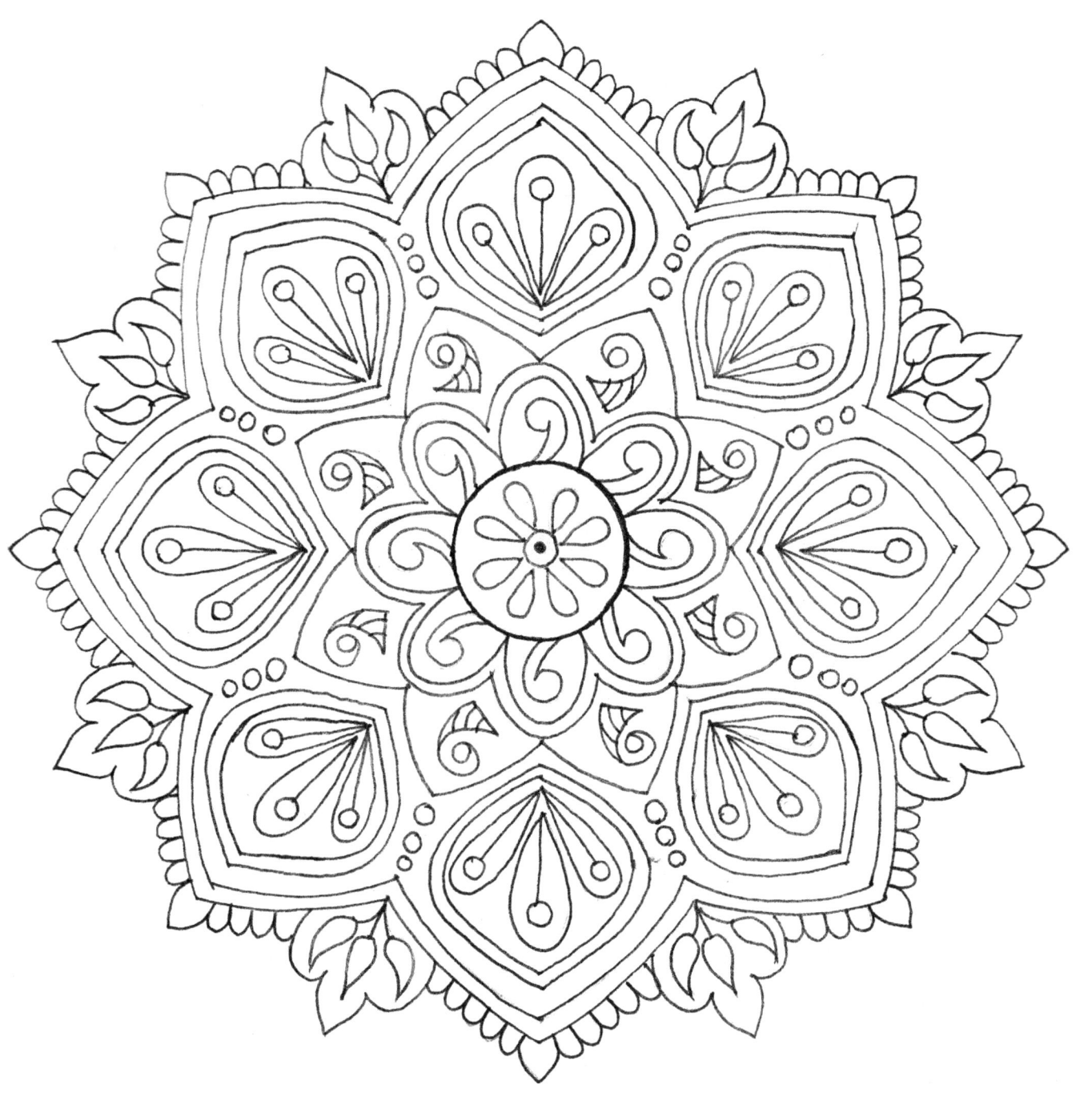

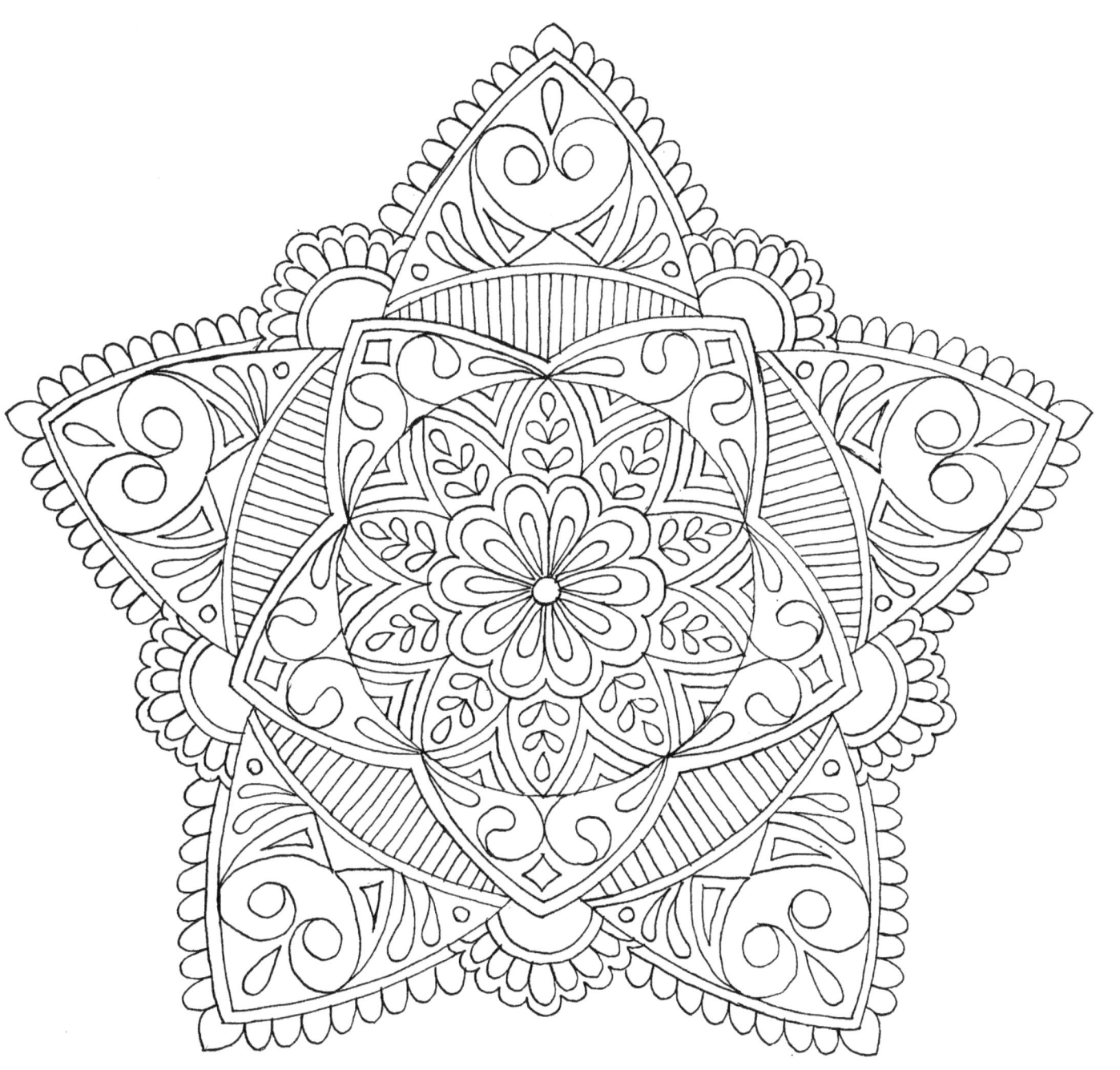

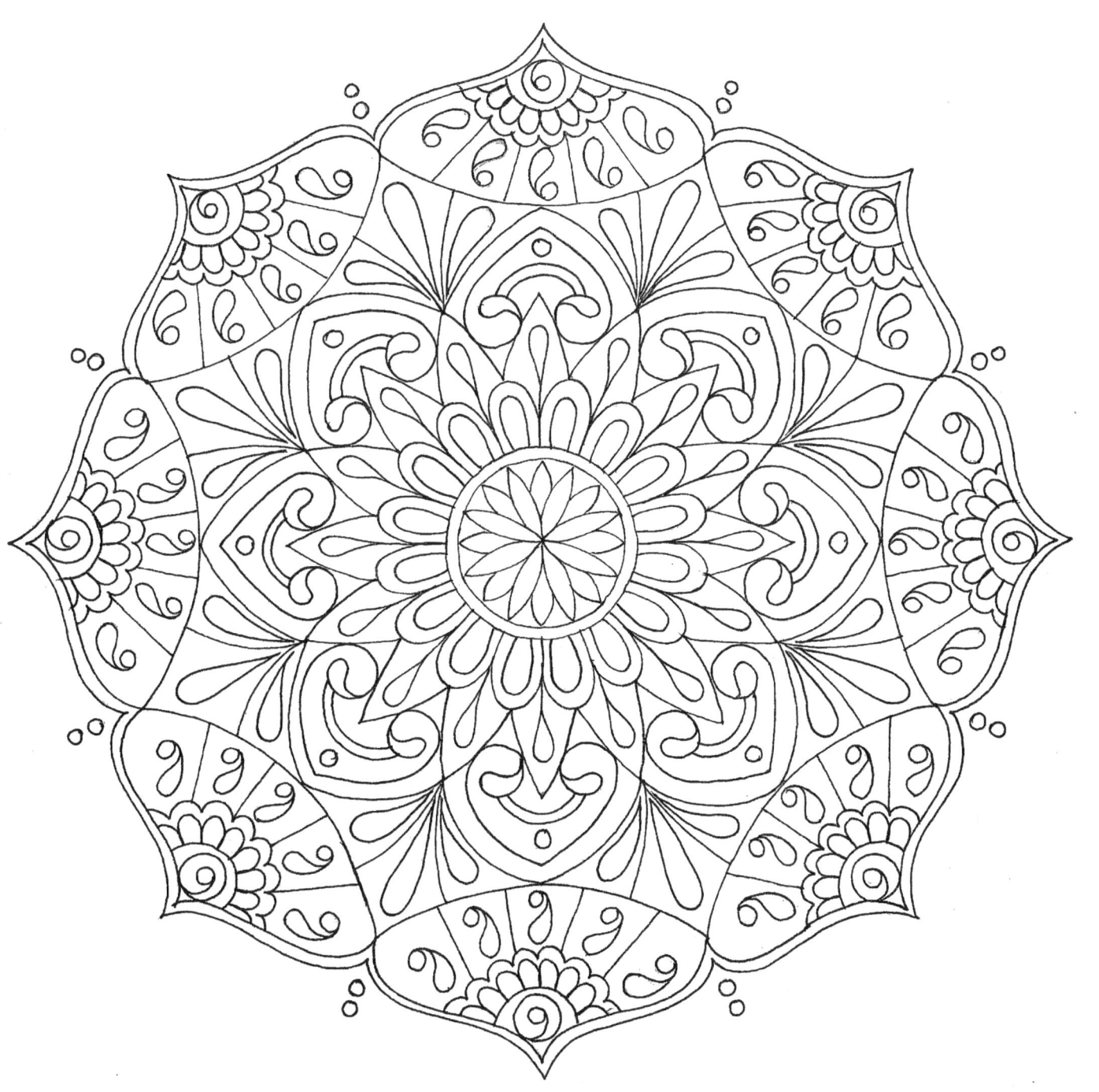

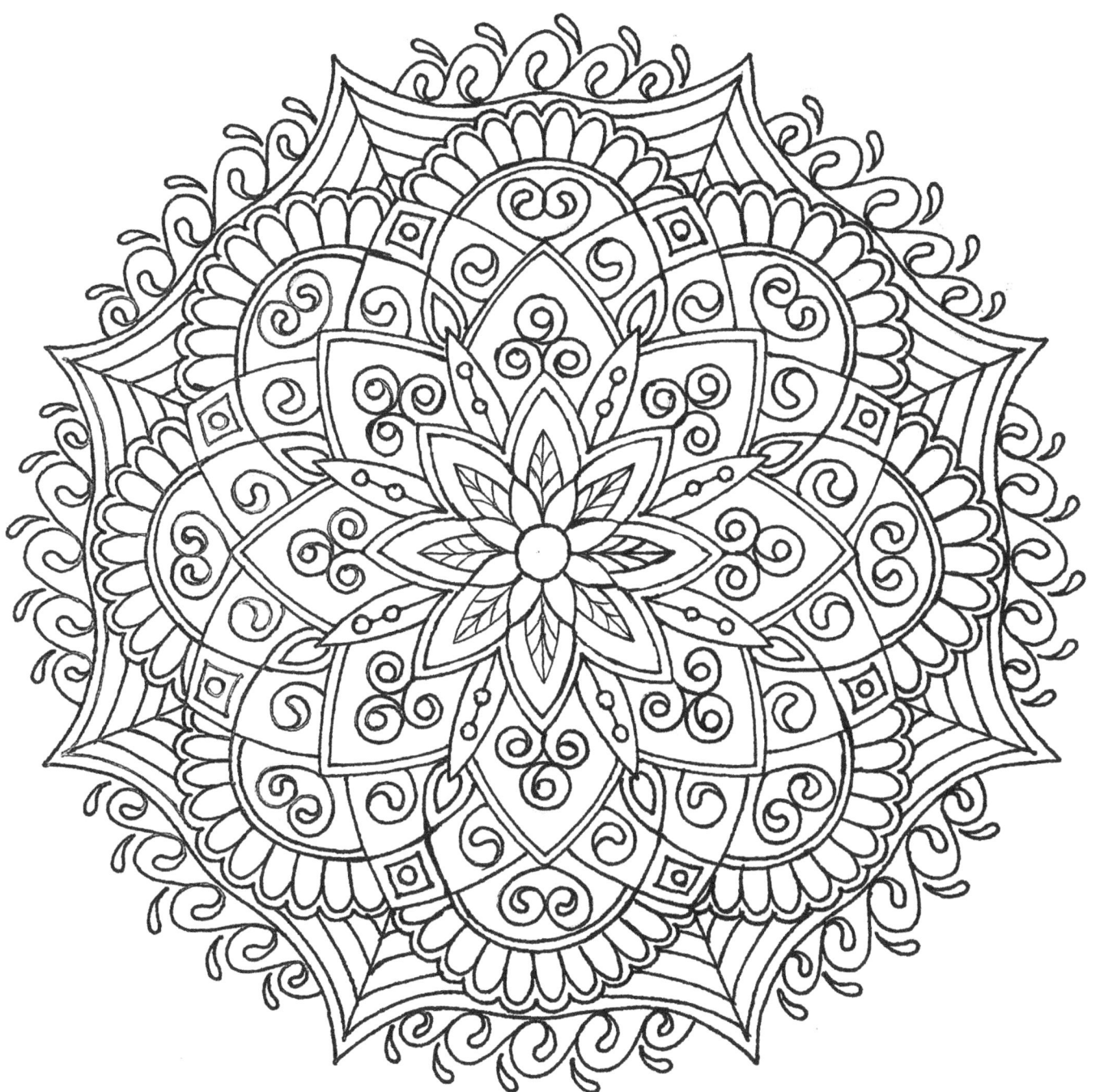

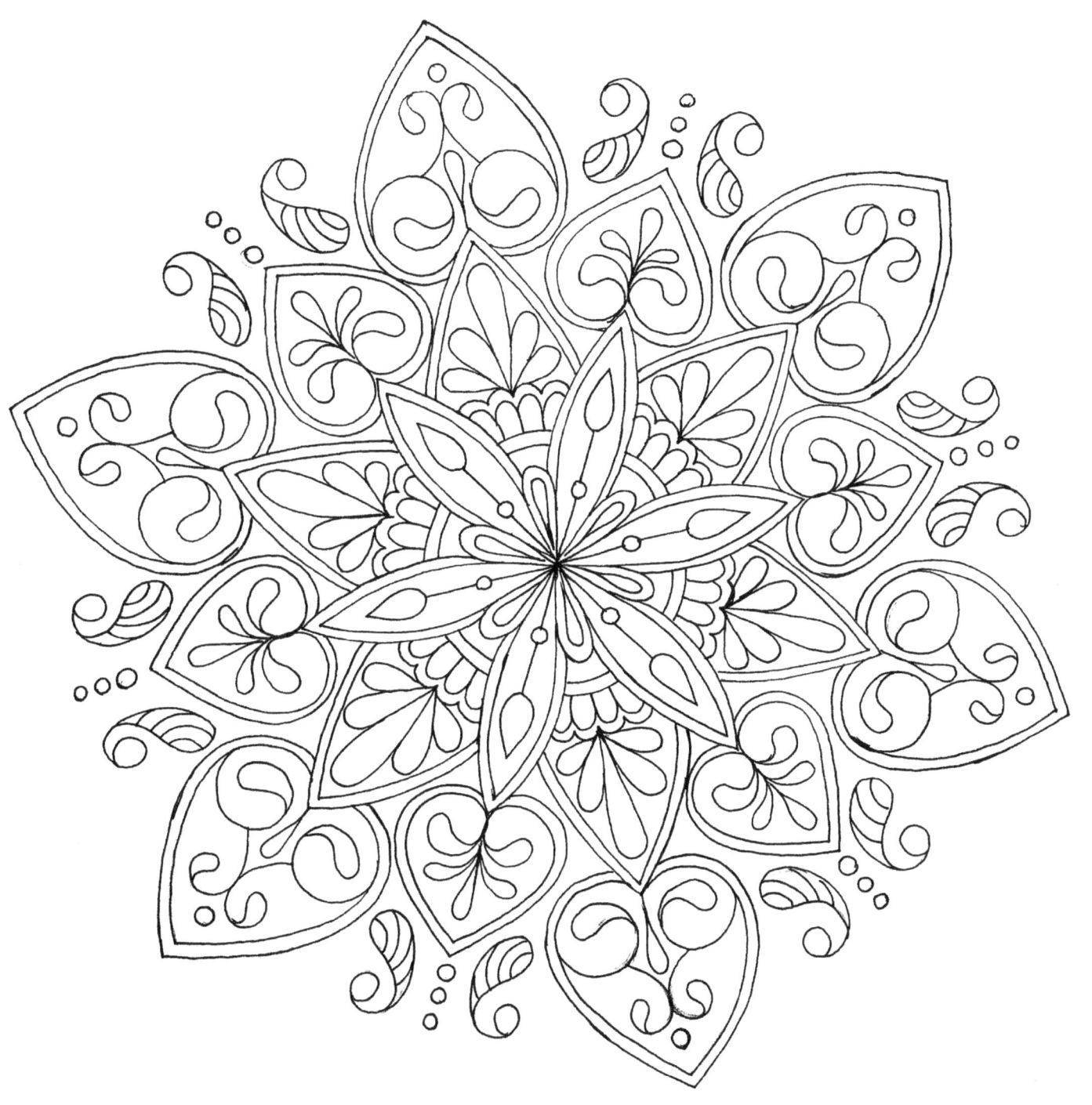

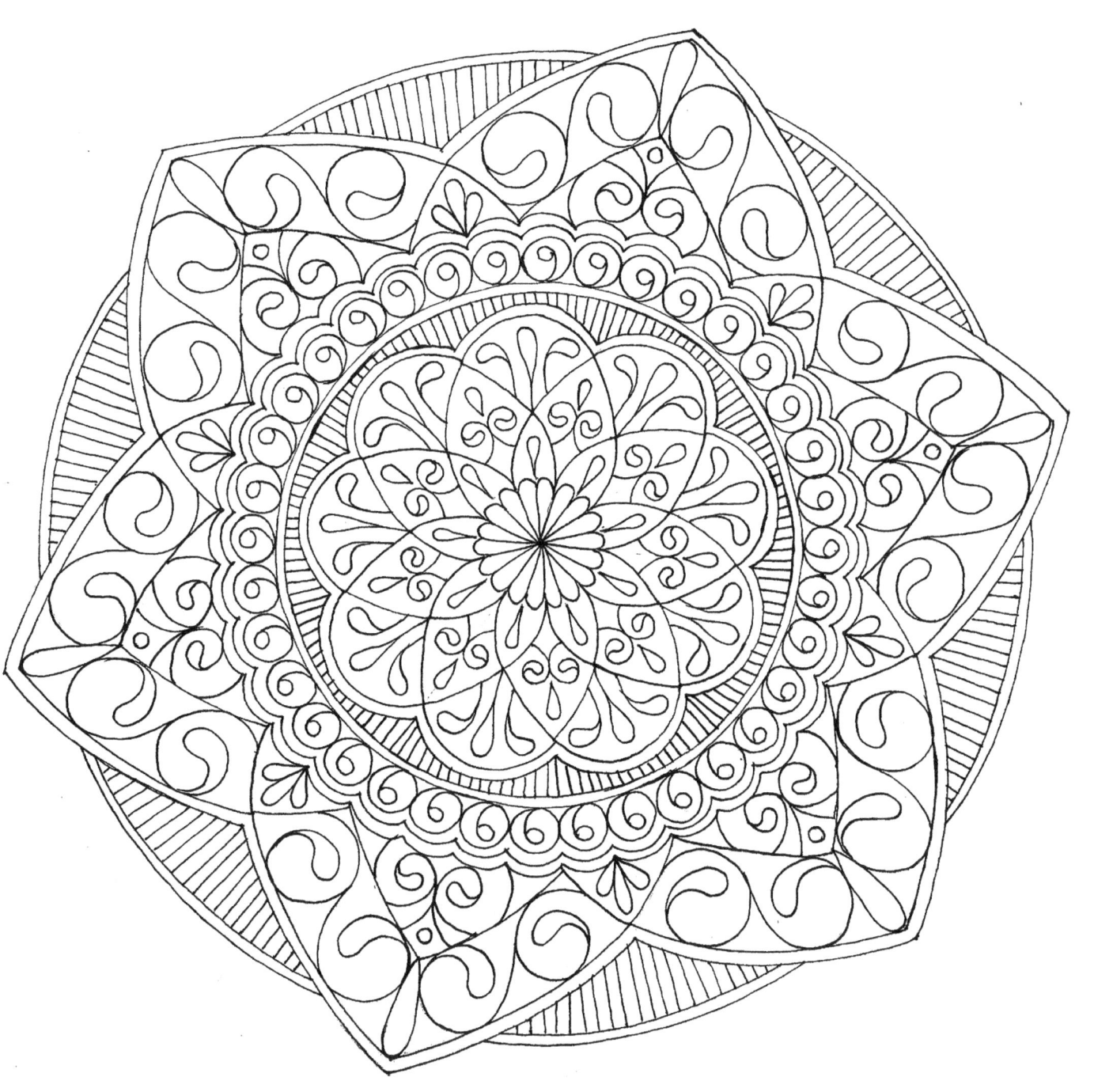

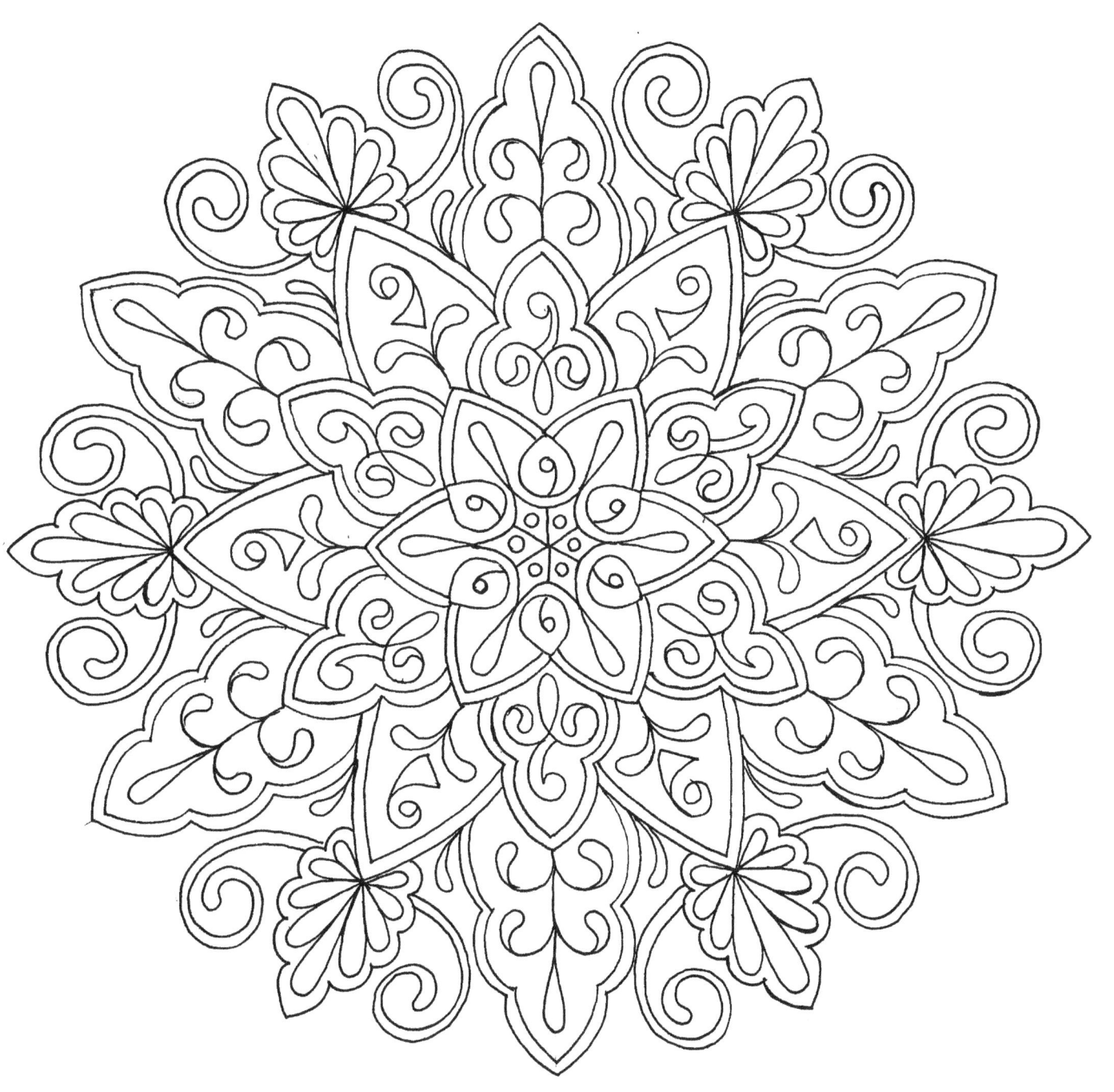

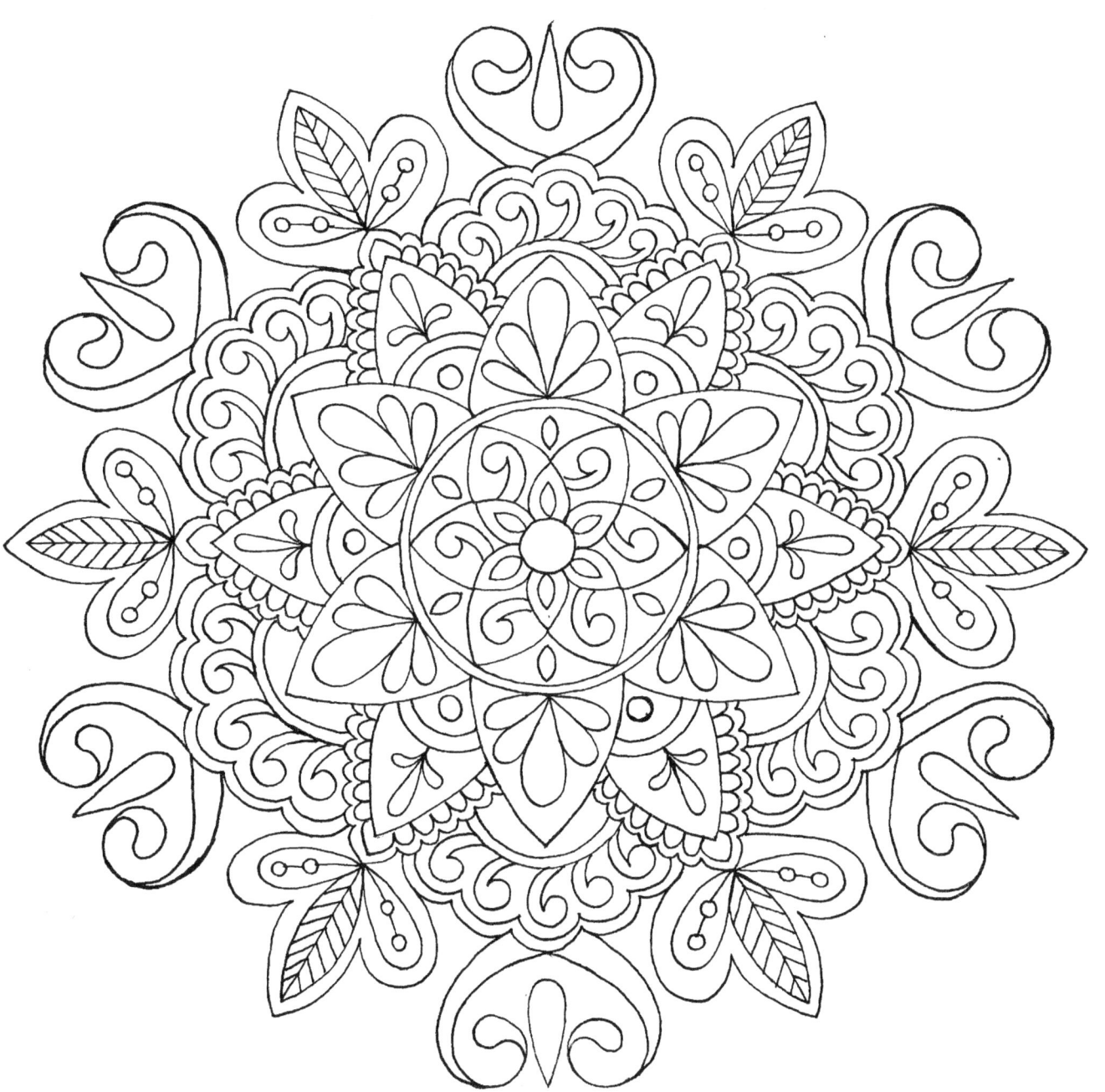

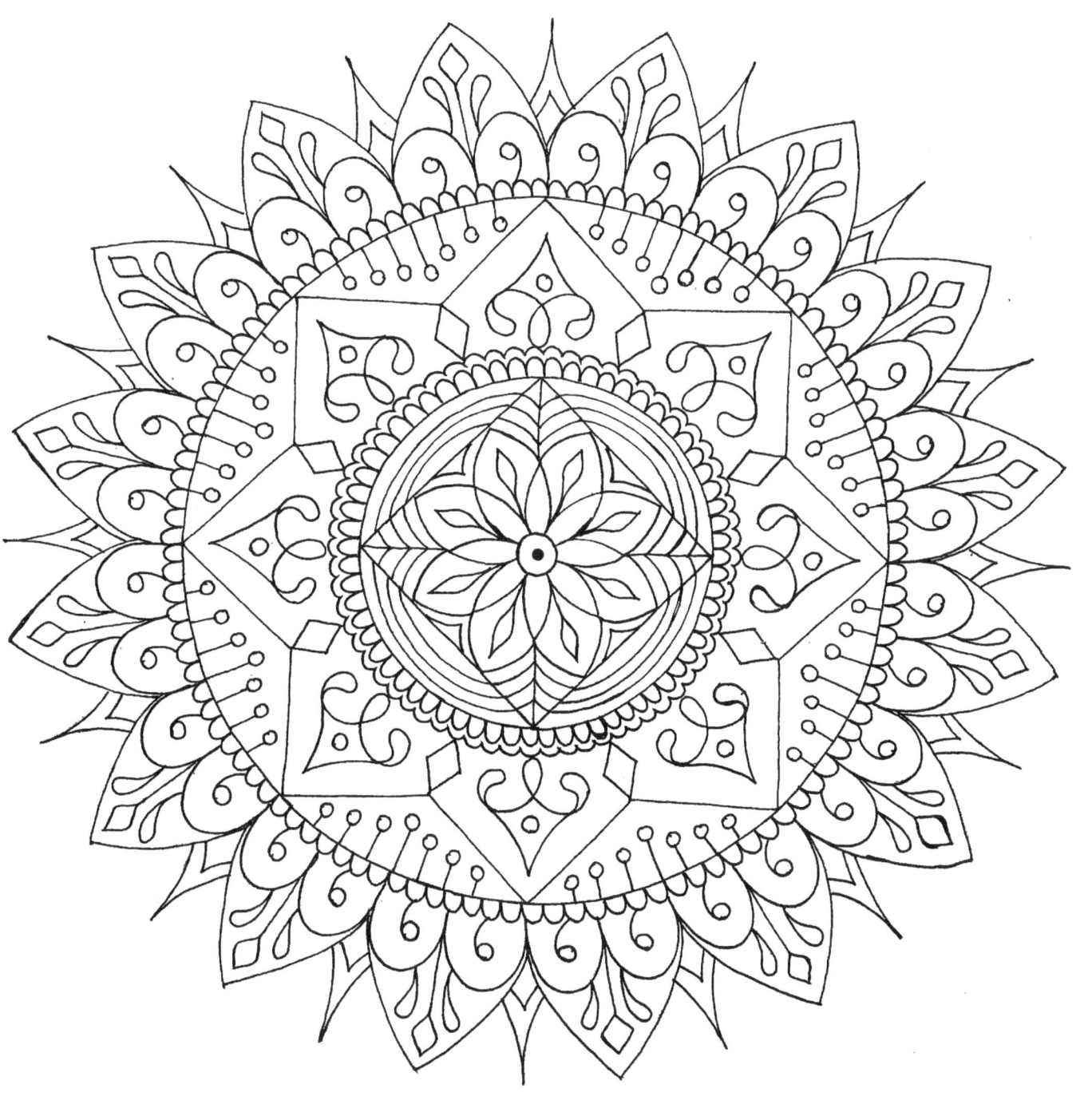

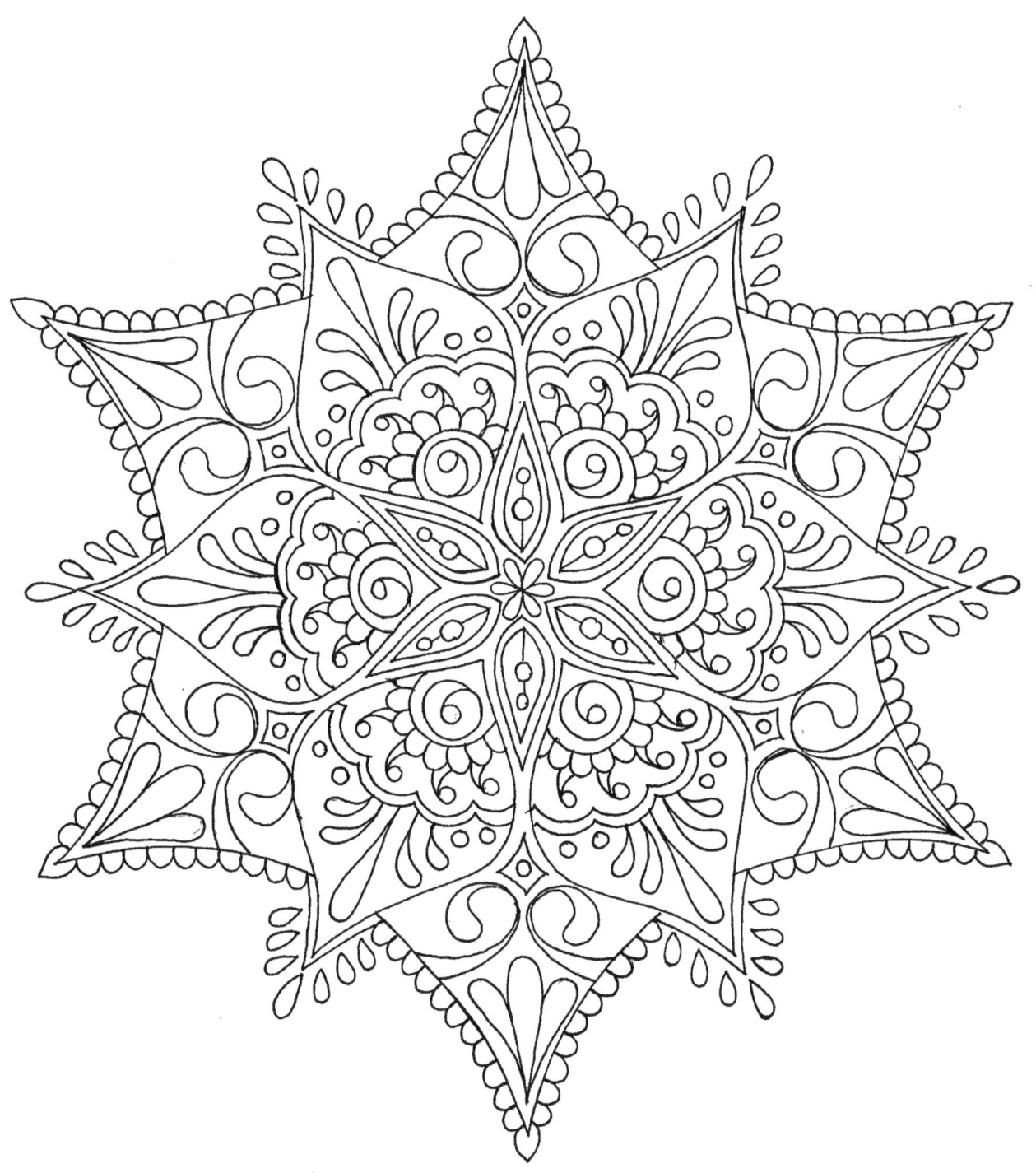

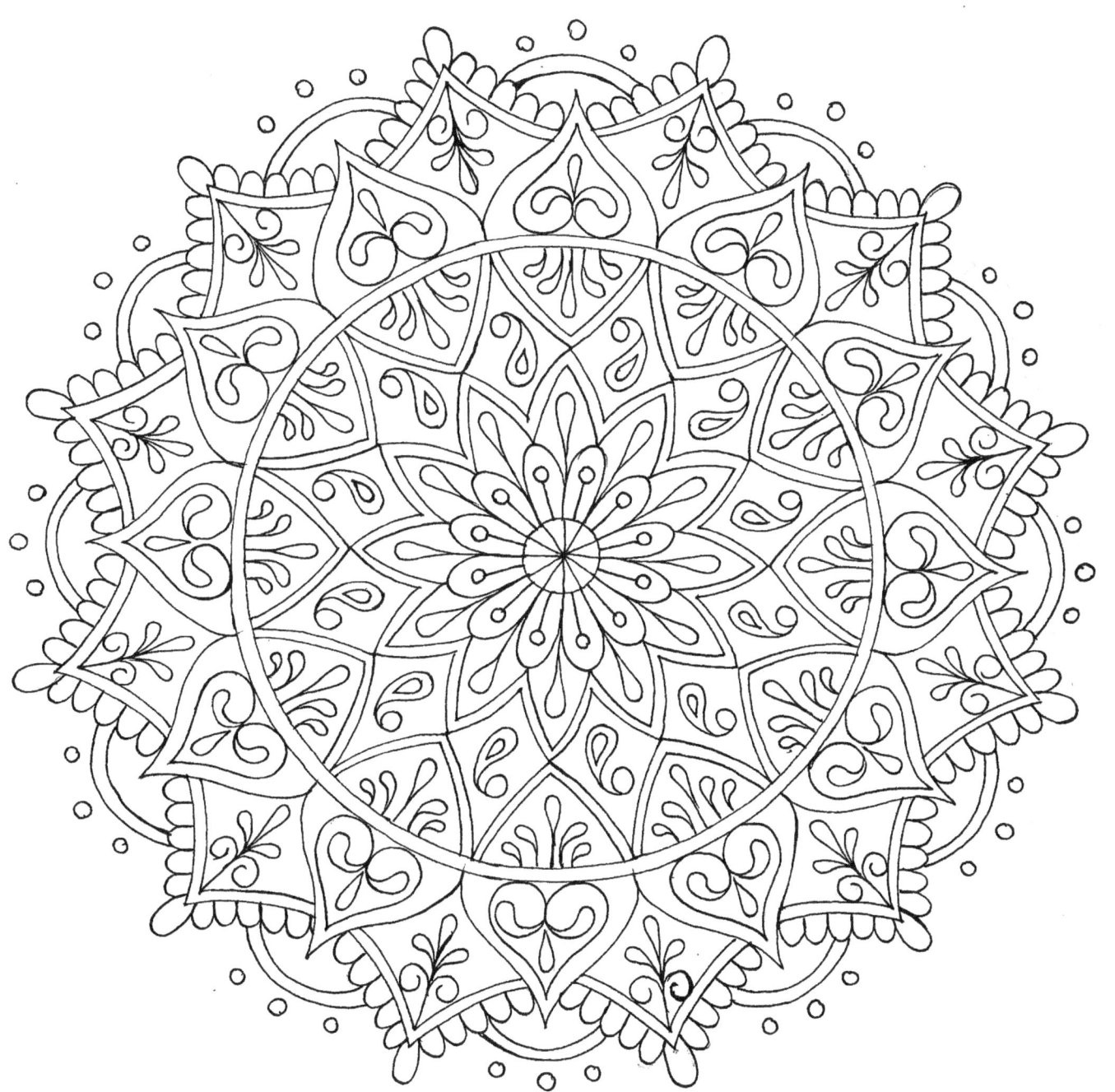

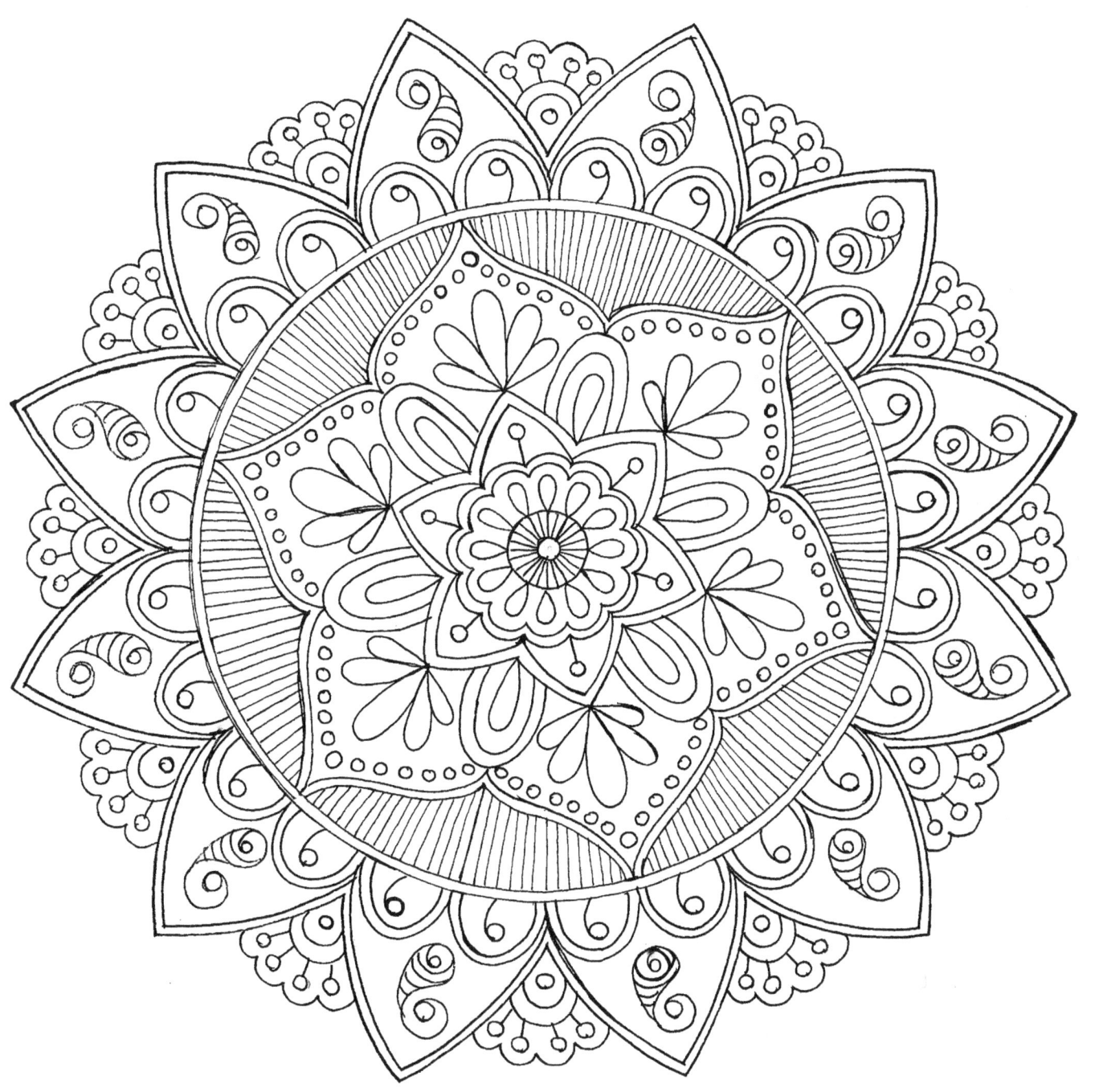

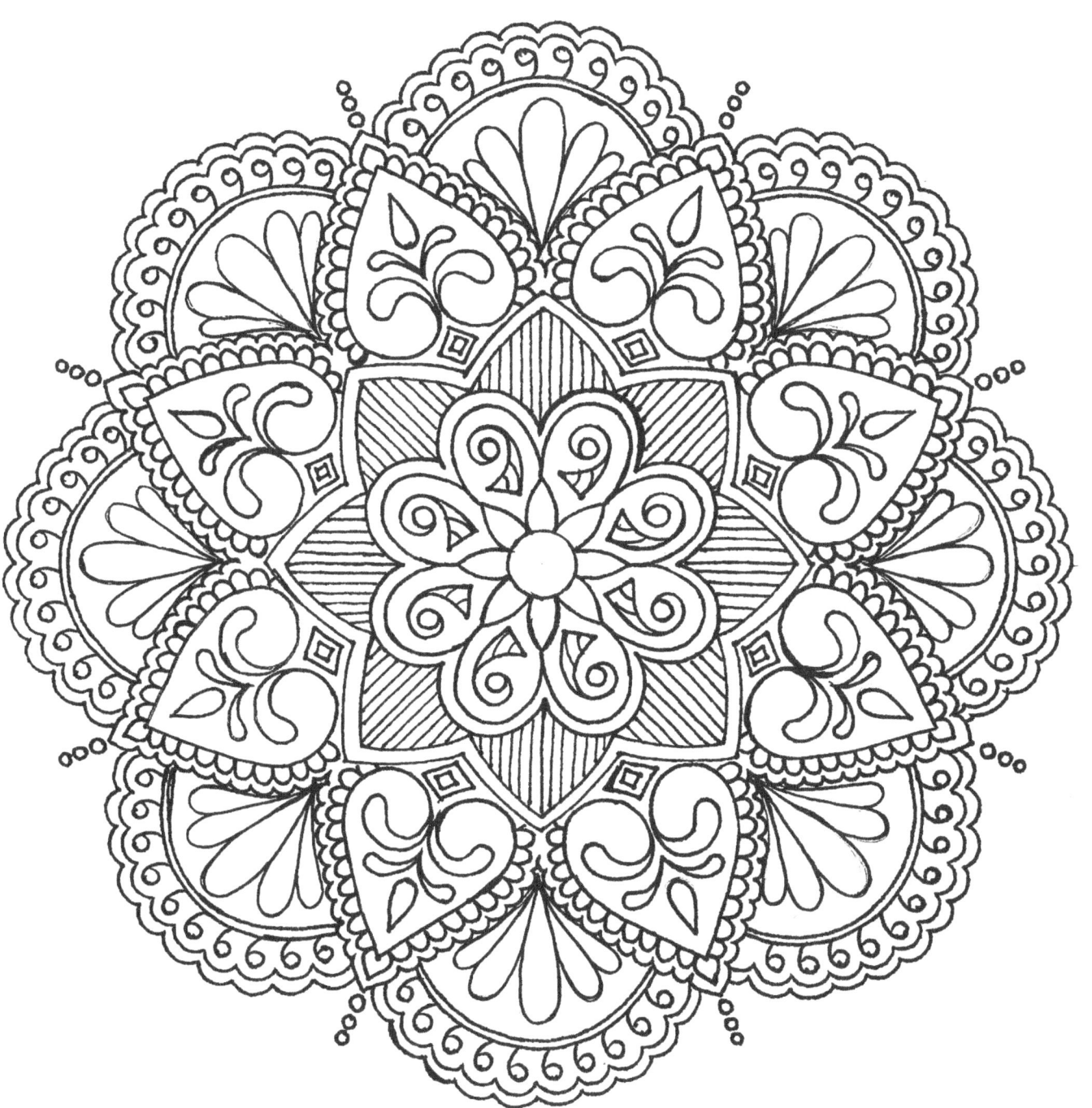

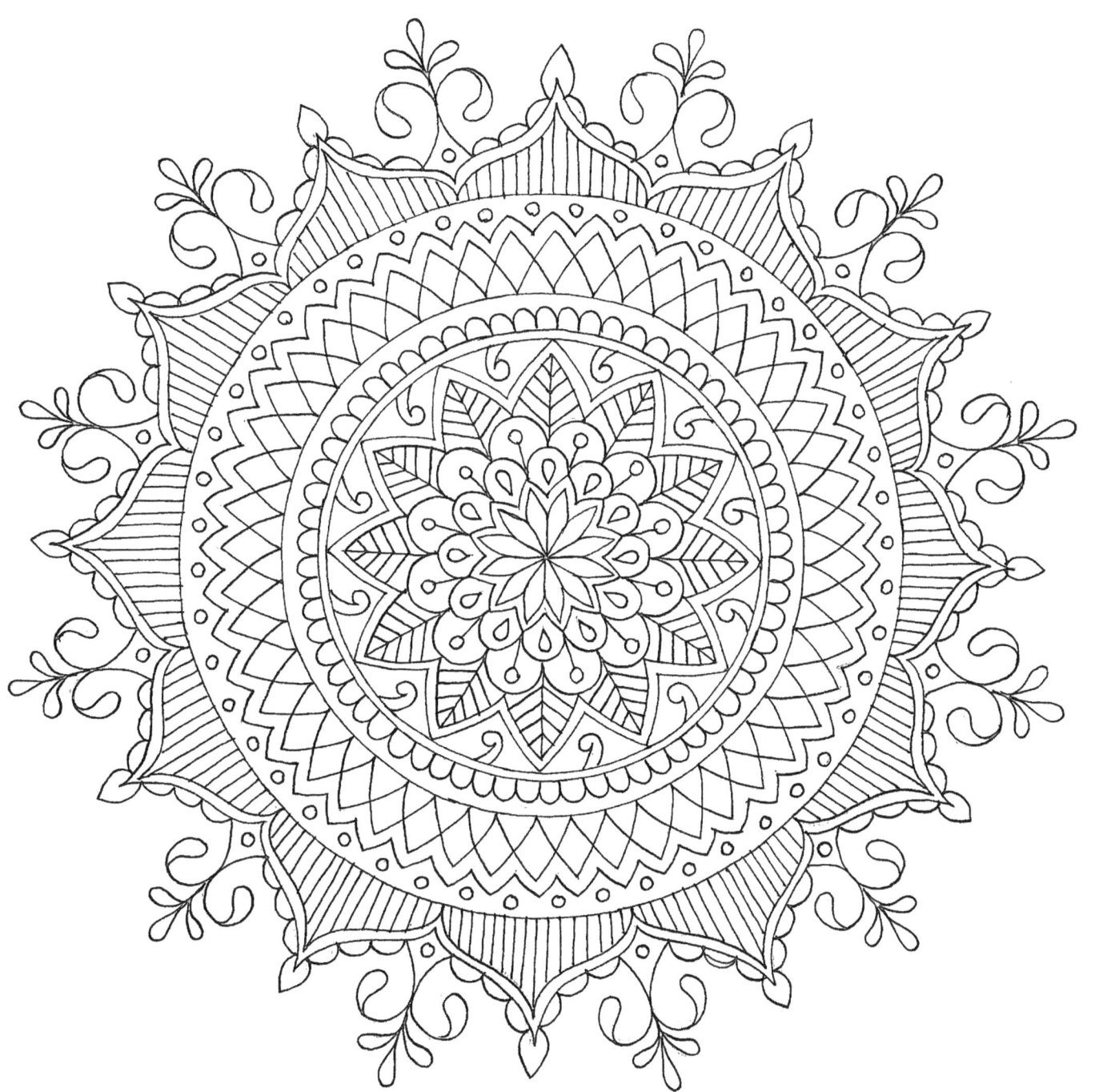

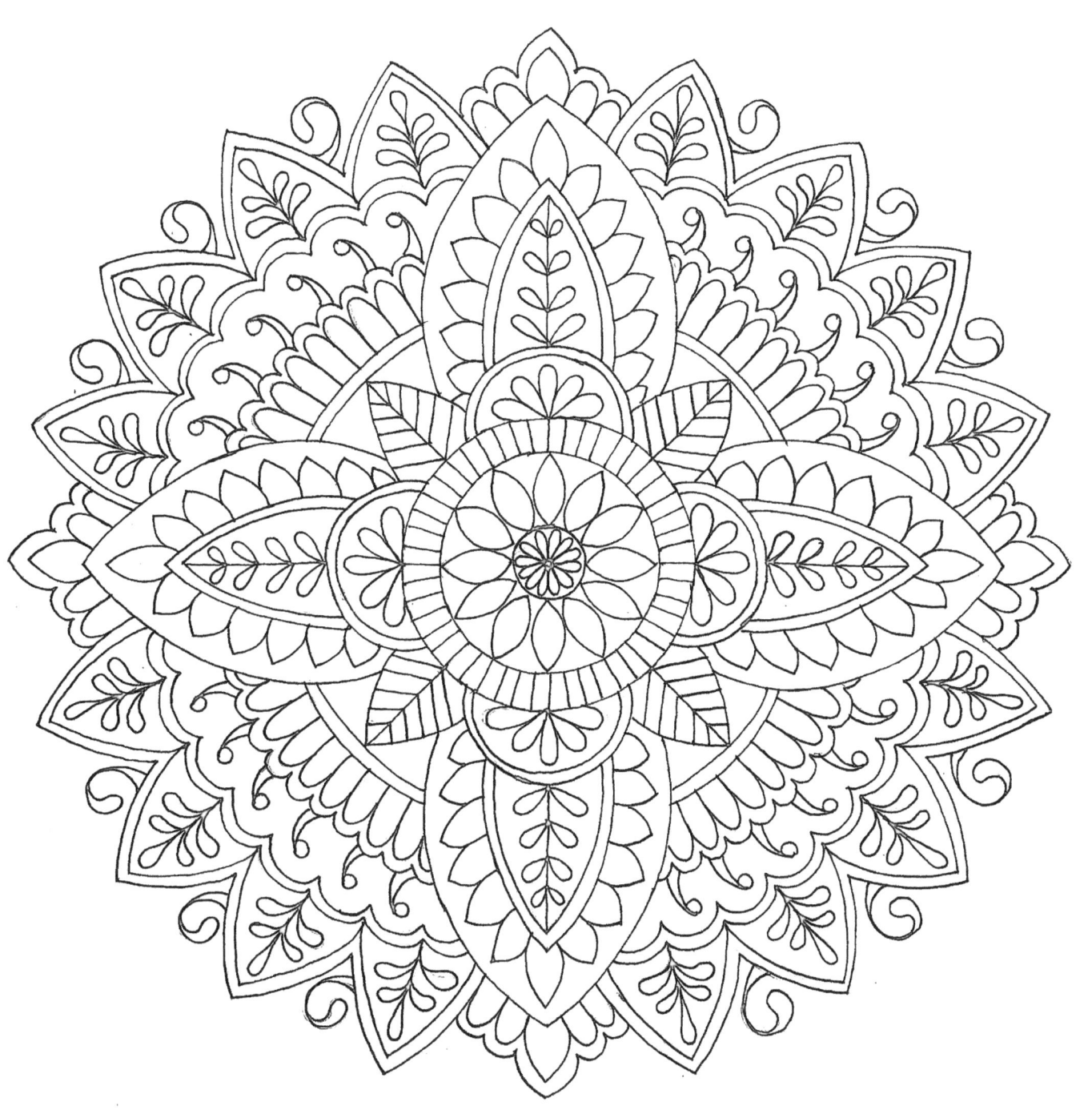

www.ingramcontent.com/pod-product-compliance
Lightning Source LLC
Chambersburg PA
CBHW060007230526
45472CB00008B/1983